Flashes of Consciousness

AF624695

Drew Campbell

BookLeaf Publishing

Presentation by *BookLeaf Publishing*

Web: www.bookleafpub.com

E-mail: info@bookleafpub.com

ISBN: 9789357445443

First edition 2021

DEDICATION

I dedicate this book to those who have believed in me through my endless creative journey.

ACKNOWLEDGEMENT

Firstly, I would like to thank my partner, Monica, for her endless support and tolerance for my outlandish and otherworldly ideas. I honestly don't believe I would have come this far if it weren't for her.

Also, thanks to all of my family and friends who kept believing in me throughout my creative journey.

PREFACE

Flashes of Consciousness can be found when you are not even looking...

Floating

A requiem for the future,
Bet all odds on today.
A broken existence,
Forgiven with riches.
Alone,
Till my message is reached.
Alive,
Till misfortune mistook me.
Afraid.
The feeling everything is built upon.
Another station achieved.
Showering down,
The lies forgotten with time.
One exists,
Apart from the stems.

Apart

The day sets,
Usual as always
Though the sun rises, anew.
Unfamiliar, and disconnected.
Away from the known universe.
Everyone,
Displeased with the notion,
That we do not understand.
Etherical,
Off to another land.
Broken…
Splinters…
Fractures in the mind…

From Within

Truth,
An exhaustion of time.
Spirits left alone.
A will of leaving,
Set plainly.

But an inheritance,
Shrouding its existence.
Seals a warning, blatantly.
Away from what hearts intend.
Clouds of chaos, unspoken.
And the will acts too late.

Shadows

Existing,
Though everyone forbids it.
Outcasts of the natural rhythm.
Laid traumatized, and at risk.
Broken, yet living.
Breaths ahead of the future.
Frightened of the failure,
Inevitable…
Sorcery succumbs,
to the shadows cast upon us.
Only a matter of time,
Before doubt reigns over.

Tomorrow

Little fragments,
Remembered out of sequence.
Blankness fills the gaps between thoughts.
The taste of bile,
Staining my entire pallet.

Piecing together facts,
Left scattered in the morning.
Embarrassment and nausea…
Unable to stomach nutrients.
The ground unstable…
Waves rushing over,
In fluid intervals.

Anger barricades,
The fortresses of comfort.
Not willing to let me come home.
Head splitting,
Water only worsening the fate.

Shifting

The freedoms allowed,
Often bring destruction.
Everyday walking in,
To an unforeseeable storm.

The order is limiting,
And may seem petty.
Though success is far greater.
The clean air,
Lends to breaths of ease.
Even slivers of excitement,
Can be found amongst the fear.

A single unit,
Operating in unison.
Each piece running their task.
Alive in each moment.
Even when the storms attack us.
Order,
          Maintained…
When the lands of past experience,
Slowly wither away.

Fabricated Rule

Shadows congregate,
Behind thin veils of subtlety.
Flaunting self-appointed supremacy.
Speaking misguided reality,
Into an unfortunate existence.

Questioning dedication,
When so much time has been wasted.
Grunt work, achieved.
Then overlooked.
Allegiance shifts,
Almost akin to disloyalty.
Though I am only a mirror.
Giving back what I am subjected to.
All is delivered.
All is right…
Almost…

Harbinger

Gliding through existence, day by day.
Achieving tiny victories,
Or large toward reformation.
Each time floating further away,
From the eclipse behind us.
Detachment from the dead-end path.

Then upon arrival, of where I am supposed to be,
A grim glimpse of severed strings,
Shows its face to the present.
Forewarning of the gloom setting in.
A speech filled with inaccurate allusions,
And the contagion of ignorance.

Settling for failure and self-destruction.
Littering unfinished downers,
Across fields of fading ruins.
Becoming one with the vermin.
Your choice to make…
But please keep it far enough away.

False Narrative

Fluttering distractions,
Dance eagerly toward us.
Seduction through sweet sounds,
And promises of leisure.
Calling you away….

Attempted bargains,
Falling flat above your head.
Stuck, and obligated to duty.
Then lies, speak softly.
Unaware,
The spirits tease, though understand.

The truth eludes them.
But a few know, or suspect,
The narrative is fragile.
Discomfort is only fiction,
As you dance with decisions.
Transparent,
And plagued with plot holes.
Respect, will slowly diminish.
Though to blind eyes,
You still shine, golden.
While the grit of the forgotten,
It becomes buried in gray…

Taken Away

Thoughts flow,
in a womb of creative spirit.
A scribe,
The vessel of its physical form.
Though focus is easily broken.
Holes threaten the hermetic world.
Air of distraction,
Breathes heavy onto developing cosmos.
The lights begin to dim.
Freeing those held at bay.
Procrastination guised as wicked creatures.
Eating away little progressions.
Ripped out of development.
Falling behind…
Now the energy is replaced with stress.
Unable to shelter our creations.
From those who threaten their existence.
Ideas become glimmers of nothing.
Memories, left hollow.
Trying desperately to remember.
The worlds are left barren…

From Many

Stars shine, disconnected.
Though rays of light combine.
Forming constellations,
Casting webs that trap ideas.
Growing them into nutrients.
Feeding off the cosmic auras.

The sky is for all to gaze at.
But its message varies to each viewer.
Perceptions from completed pictures.
Each journey, just a pixel of truth.
Possible outcomes,
Are infinite variables.
Portals intersecting throughout space.
Consciousness crossing over,
Bringing to life, new light.

Open World

Looking over a vast forest of words.
Often revisiting its wisdom.
Telling tales, sparking knowledge.

Beyond the tree line,
An infinite ocean of blank pages.
Lying under another sea of stars.
The forest,
Eagerly awaits to expand.
To become a part of this great world.

Days pass,
Still staring out into the stagnant waters.
Throwing seeds,
Only to find them wash back to shore.
I step out,
Exploring the undeveloped sea.
No discoveries, or adventures.
Just silence, and inactivity.

Caught somewhere,
Far from the lands I have created.
No way of coming back.
I dip my quill into the ocean,
Expecting nothing…

Then the still surface begins to move.
Tiny currents, sway around me.
Then waves splash onto my face.

I feel a rumble,
Far beneath my floating body.
And my feet are met by solid ground.
I slowly rise above the water.
On an island,
I stand in amazement.
Then I climb the tallest tree.

All around me,
The ocean stirs,
Awaiting to be explored.
I jump from the treetop,
Into the water off the shore.
Lifted again,
Then skipping like a stone across a pond.
New islands emerge from every jump.
I see the stars glimmer,
Almost as if pleased.

When I stop,
I look before me.
My forest just another skip away.
I could return and finish it,
But for now, I choose another path.
I skip off the other way,

Met by more new islands.
Forming new ideas,
To be saved for harvest.

Eventually,
The growth will continue again.
But as the forest patiently awaits,
I make use of each moment.
Wasting no time, and shunning no outcome.
In harmony with these worlds,
The ocean, and one day, the stars…

Expiration Date

Infinite points of origin,
All congregate in a hub.
With intentions toward betterment.
They never considered the nature of heart.
Contacting one another,
Creating this new state of normal.
Almost as if there was no life before.

Leaves fall in the water.
Flowing with the river,
Caught drifting away in the moment.
No concept of an ending.
But this stream only takes us so far.
Is there any chance beyond the edge?

Expiration is the fate of all that lives.
This idea of permanence is a laughable fantasy.
I cannot begin to know your wishes.
And I required, only one last entanglement.
A final step that would seem pointless later on.
It was perfect, for what it was.
A trivial tangent, from the desired path.

To Reach the Sky

Synchronized pitch icicles ascending from a
barren field.
Planted in a thoughtless garden, that all else
shall yield.
Unified amongst their own, they proudly wear
the lifeless mark.
Instill in all the masses, that you will bow and
fear their bark.
High above the current's pulling, their tribe, they
are the loudest.
Their synthesized dark shadows, combine and
nearly shroud us.
But no thoughts that elude them, can find home
in this sward.
Just as their bitter calling, cannot find home in
this separated shard.

Synchronized in every evil, planted in this
barren field.
Thoughtless as the plastic daggers, their
weakened arms still wield.
Argue for self-preservation, although they are
the drones.
Compensation for the lack of something, are the
static tones.

Crying out to the Gods of Fools, begging them for courage.
Though synthesized, is the already meaningless pledge.
No mind separate from each other, they swallow the foolish.
Identical are the faces of filth, synchronized in every wish.

False steam is carried into our breathing, causing us to hear.
Heard through darkness are their voices, though they are not near.
Pitiful abominations, are the arguments of their false rule.
Exhaling the source of judgment, screaming through a web of drool.
Unaware of their own vices, still on top, they're in denial.
Fire pierces the white cover, burning us, but not the vile.
All over the planet's beauty, poisonous dark fluids leak.
They tell us of our misfortune, they the children of the weak.

Wasted energy assembles in the desert sand.
Time slows and the flames of dimness are fanned.

They possess no feathered wings to spread and fly
The pointless static vessels attempt to reach the sky.

Time to Rewrite

The flow of time,
Neatly unspools,
As the events we follow take place.
Passengers on a great adventure,
Take the invisible reigns.
Then time pauses,
And slowly retracts the past few moments.
Our heroic team of four,
Now only three.
The quiet one,
Is no longer.
Events unfold once again.
Differently than before…

Time halts again…
New details come to light,
As others are lost.
Soon, a third and final stop.
Characters remain suspended in time.
Nothing progresses…
The reigns they once held,
Reveal themselves as strings,
Pulled by an indecisive master.

Sold Resources

A pawn,
Given false command,
Of an untrained army.
Exploited for his cheap labor.
No ambitions,
His time drained into a falling vessel.
While each day,
He also drowns himself.

A good heart,
Stopped beating.
The day the anchor clenched it.
Chains slowly tearing in.
Blood now pumped,
Through dishonest machines.
Smiling as they lie.

A council,
Moving fate.
To secure their own.
Though filth rots their paradise.
And it will be found.
Exposed.
And put back in order.

Accusations and Actuality

The dullness eludes.
Keepers of our livelihood
Turning them petty.

Having what we want
Mistaken for what we need.
Looking out for me.

Your intent reflects
That which you accuse me of.
Eat the food given.

If I am needed,
Then you will call upon me.
Cast out, until then.

Consistent Paradox

Alarms,
Coming in all forms.
Breaking continuity.
Each verse,
A variation of the source.

A shape,
With infinite sides.
A sphere at its core.
Projecting light in all directions.
Forming parallel worlds.

Energy,
Flowing between them all.
Clouds of cosmic thought.
We arise from our suppression.
Holding claim to our creation.
Cherishing what we have found.
Forgetting those,
Who held us down.

Retroactive

Events laid out neatly.
Linking up perfectly in a chain.
Aligned and interwoven.
Each moment evolving,
Into another.

A superior scribe sits upon,
An unquestioned throne.
Overseeing the worlds as they orbit.
Displeased with the details present.
Not the broad strokes of his predecessor,
But the blocks placed by his peers.

Cracks are created, forming questions.
Confused by which are true.
Layers of uncertainty, build toward
incompletion.
Though there is always the question of the
portal.
A path toward an answer.
Not hidden, just unconsidered.

A vast array of moons,
Orbit around infinite suns.
Drifting through this plain of stars.

Each with several variations.
Between them all, are many thoughts.
We may never know which truth to follow.
Each, just an interpretation.
Disregarding the others.

Foci

Elaborate illustrations,
Pieces drawn with words.
Creating pictures in the mind.
Conscious thoughts,
Flash before the eyes.
Rapidly changing lives.

Two points,
Anchored across reality.
Emerging simultaneously.
Speaking to diverse ears.
Separated through space,
But the two linked by their spirit.
Each half of a complete message.

Forces bringing down the stars.
Hailing fire, to ignite a cause.
Reactions boil across the empty sky.
The wellspring at the center point.
Answers to questions we ask ourselves.
Is this a valid path?

A jump forward,
Both feet landing.
Waiting to take their separate steps.

Mountains growing toward one another.
With little rivers in between them.
Flowing in impossible directions.

A planet, unrecognizable.
A fabricated home,
Comprised of our thoughts and motions.
Seizing power over ourselves.
Bringing forth evolutions.
Leaving behind our stagnant dreams.

Accepting a new set of ambitions.
We cease to be imposters.
The strength was there, just untapped.
Filtered through expectations.
Rational choices can finally occur.
All starting with the two…

Ceaselessly Shaping

A world completed.
Down to the last pixel,
          Locked in time.
Stories unfold in the vastness of the universe.
Causes,
Effect outcomes.
Life's complex pleasures.

Growth,
          Ceaseless...
A constant state of unraveling.
Even states of existence,
Welcome open challenges.
As if wanting to be rewritten.
Logic evolves,
Contradicting obsolete functions,
Battling to build further.

Factors generated, and alive.
Proudly we gaze as it matures, and thrives.

Complexion,
Rooting further inward,
And exploding outward.
Energy shifting currents.

Adaptability is the source.
Conducting intricate patches.
Forging consistency.
A source of infinite outcomes,
Scattered throughout time.
Cracks between established borders,
Like wounds when in infancy.
Soon become scars of narrative.
Scribes consider all.
Flashes of consciousness,
Overlap in a pixelated view.
But from a distance,
There is more clarity.
The fabric is stitched with warming layers.
Complicated in just its structure.

Not factoring in,
The sky, land, and wind…

Each with their own story to tell.
Chambers open up,
Throughout reality.
Little rooms and realms come alive.
Building new textures across the plains.
Annual glitches,
Now a natural phenomenon.
Abiding by no laws that are consistent,
But unique to each venture.
Many unseen…

The vast existence,
Only allows focus with limited scope.
History, only a sliver,
Of the entire story.
Therefore, infinitely swaying.
Creating extensions…

Lights from all angles,
Forming shapes between the structures.
Elements growing inward.
New discoveries,
Both molecular and cosmic,
Strengthen each limb,
As we jump between them.
Splintering,
Till there is no blank canvas.
Reaching far beyond the medium.
Eyes opening,
And seeing colors glow in darkness.
The cold air,
Is a whisper from beyond understanding.
Breathing forever, from each shadow.
Casting light,
Waiting to be found…

www.ingramcontent.com/pod-product-compliance
Lightning Source LLC
Chambersburg PA
CBHW051750130826
49812CB00033B/1083
* 9 7 8 9 3 5 7 4 4 5 4 4 3 *